E.J.; Eastman Wilber

Treatise on Counterfeit, Altered, and Spurious Bank Notes

E.J.; Eastman Wilber

Treatise on Counterfeit, Altered, and Spurious Bank Notes

ISBN/EAN: 9783742863140

Manufactured in Europe, USA, Canada, Australia, Japa

Cover: Foto ©Andreas Hilbeck / pixelio.de

Manufactured and distributed by brebook publishing software
(www.brebook.com)

E.J.; Eastman Wilber

Treatise on Counterfeit, Altered, and Spurious Bank Notes

A

TREATISE

ON

COUNTERFEIT, ALTERED, AND SPURIOUS

BANK NOTES,

WITH

UNERRING RULES FOR THE DETECTION OF FRAUDS IN THE SAME.

Illustrated with Original Steel, Copper, and Wood Plate Engravings,

PREPARED EXPRESSLY FOR THIS WORK.

TOGETHER WITH

A HISTORY OF ANCIENT MONEY, CONTINENTAL CURRENCY, BANKS, BANKING,
BANK OF ENGLAND, OUR AMERICAN BANK-NOTE COMPANIES,
AND OTHER VALUABLE INFORMATION AS TO

MONEY.

BY E. J. WILBER & E. P. EASTMAN.

POUGHKEEPSIE, N. Y.:
PUBLISHED FOR THE AUTHORS.
1865.

PRICE, TWO DOLLARS.

                                                                          PAGE
5TH, NEOK,... 31
  6TH, ARMS, HANDS, AND FEET,... 31
  7TH, DRAPERY, ... 32
LANDSCAPES,... 32
LANDSCAPES, GENUINE AND COUNTERFEIT,................................. 33
DOMESTIC ANIMALS, GENUINE,.. 33
DOMESTIC ANIMALS, COUNTERFEIT,...................................... 34
BIRDS, GENUINE AND COUNTERFEIT,..................................... 34
PERSPECTIVE, GENUINE AND COUNTERFEIT,............................... 34
ARCHITECTURE, SHIPS, AND RAILROAD CARS, GENUINE AND COUNTERFEIT,..... 35
LETTERING, GENUINE,... 35
LETTERING, COUNTERFEIT,... 36
PRINTING, GENUINE,.. 36
PRINTING, COUNTERFEIT,.. 37
INK, GENUINE AND COUNTERFEIT,....................................... 37
ENGRAVER'S IMPRINT,... 38
SIGNATURES,... 38
ALTERED BANK-NOTES,... 40
PHOTOGRAPHED BILLS,... 42
FRACTIONAL CURRENCY,.. 43
GENUINE VIGNETTE AND PORTRAIT,...................................... 44
COUNTERFEIT VIGNETTE AND PORTRAIT,.................................. 44
GENUINE GEOMETRICAL LATHE-WORK,..................................... 45
COUNTERFEIT GEOMETRICAL LATHE-WORK,................................. 45
GENUINE MEDALLION RELIEF-WORK,...................................... 46
COUNTERFEIT MEDALLION RELIEF-WORK,.................................. 46
GENUINE LETTERING,.. 46
COUNTERFEIT LETTERING,.. 46
RECAPITULATION,... 48
VISIT TO THE AMERICAN BANK NOTE COMPANY.

O.M.J

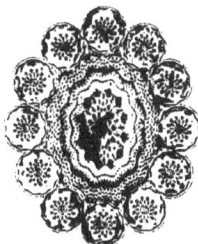

TWO

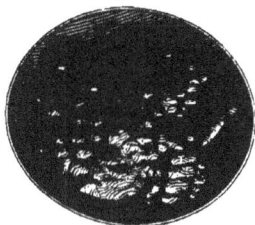

ONE

FIFTY

MONEY.

"Put money in thy purse," was the crafty advice of Iago; and from time past memory the world has adopted and acted on this happy suggestion. Not that in the "guinea's stamp," in itself considered, there is hidden any such talismanic virtue, but simply because society has adopted the piece of stamped metal as its most convenient medium for facilitating exchanges.

The oxen with which Diomede paid for his armor, the iron currency of Sparta, the belt of wampum of the North American Indian, answered the same purpose as do now the bank-bill or the gold eagle.

As individual wants become more varied and numerous, the necessity for a convenient circulating medium, not as property, but as the *representative* of property, becomes correspondingly great; and as the result of this advanced civilization, we see the whole machinery of Government, every department of society, working by means of these forces, so insignificant in themselves —Guineas, Eagles, Dollars. These constitute in themselves the Trinity in which all believe. None are so incredulous as to doubt the mission of money; none repudiate the "Almighty Dollar."

Nor can it be regarded as extravagant to say that the whole fabric of society, and of national and individual opulence, resting as it does to so great an extent on this metallic and paper basis, will stand securely only so long as confidence exists in the purity and substantiality of that basis.

The objections to a purely "hard money" or metallic circulating medium which so readily suggest themselves to every business man, have given increased importance to banks and bank-bills, and accordingly, by an almost universal custom, bank-bills are received and treated as money, in the business of life, in the making of exchange, and in all the details of a business community.

The commanding importance of moneyed institutions, in their relations to modern society, justify the observation of a distinguished American critic, that as temples were the banks of Greece, banks are the temples of America. The chief objection which is made, or can be made to a paper currency, is the facility with which, in the present state of engraving, the issues of banks may be counterfeited or altered.

The extent to which "bills" are received, and the frequency of counterfeited or altered bills, justify, as it seems, the publication of the system of rules given in the following pages for the detection of frauds in these particulars. It is estimated that there are in circulation at the present time nearly four thousand counterfeit or fraudulent bills upon banks of the United States and Canada.

ANCIENT MONEY.

Before the invasion of Julius Cæsar, the natives of England had tin plates and rings which were received as money. On the authority of Seneca, a curious account is given, where leather, appropriately stamped to give it a certain legal character, was the only current money. At a comparatively recent date in the annals of Europe, Frederick the Second, at the siege of Milan, actually paid his troops in leather money. Nearly the same circumstance occurred in England during the great wars of the barons.

The crown of Queen Philippa, which had been pawned at Cologne for £2,500, was redeemed by sending over three hundred and thirty-four sacks of wool. In the course of 1250, King John, for the ransom of his royal person, promised to pay Edward III., of England, three millions of gold crowns. In order to fulfil the obligation he was reduced to the mortifying necessity of paying the expenses of the palace in leather money, in the centre of each piece being a bright point of silver. In that reign is found the origin of the travestied honor of boyhood called conferring a leather medal. The imposing ceremonies accompanying a presentation gave full force, dignity, and value to a leather jewel, which noblemen were probably proud and grateful to receive at the hands of Majesty.

As late as 1574, there was an immense issue of money in Holland, stamped on small sheets of pasteboard. But farther back in the vista of years, Numa Pompilius, the second king of Rome, who reigned six hundred and twenty-two years before the Christian era, made money out of wood as well as leather.

Both gold and silver appear to have been in extensive circulation in Egypt soon after their potency was understood in Asia. Thence they were introduced into Carthage and Greece, and finally, travelling farther and farther in a westerly direction, Rome discovered the importance of legalizing their circulation as money.

Weight having always been of the first importance in early times, the shape of money appears to have been a matter of perfect indifference for a series of years. When the small pieces or portions of metal received as precious were extensively circulated, it is quite probable that each person shaped them to suit his own convenience, as is practised to some extent at this time, in remote portions of the East Indies. There the payer cuts off parts with shears, till he obtains by exact weight the stipulated price. It was thus that men travelled with the evidence of their possessions in a sack. But great inconvenience must have resulted from this often tedious process, and as nations advanced in civilization and the economic arts, a certain mark or impression on pieces of certain size caused them to be acknowledged each as the representative of a certain sum of money. This facilitated negotiations, and afterward led to further improvements both in the shape, weight, and beauty of the external devices. The custom which has prevailed for a long series of years, in all the nations of Europe, of stamping the medallion likeness of the reigning sovereign on the coin newly issued, enables us to read the history of their successive dynasties in the faces on the national currency. So that the "stamped metal" answers a twofold purpose. The "guinea's stamp" becomes a history in itself, which, as Hood sings,

> "———Even its minted coins express ;
> Now stamped with the image of good Queen Bess,
> And now of a bloody Mary."

CONTINENTAL CURRENCY.

Money as well as patriotism is needed for the defence of any country. In the contest which established American Independence, patriotism was not lacking, but the money, in many instances, was lamentably deficient. The Congress of the United States experienced great difficulty in providing the requisite means for carrying on hostilities, and, to supply this want, May 10th, 1775, soon after the battle of Lexington, Congress made preparations to issue three millions of Continental Paper, two millions of which was put in circulation on June 22d following.

When first issued, this money was everywhere at par, and

proved of great utility to the army and country generally. In 1790, when nearly three millions had been issued, it began to depreciate. Rumors gained circulation that Congress would not redeem these bills, which, although promptly denied, caused great loss to holders. Forty dollars of this money would bring but one of gold or silver, and the evil was aggravated by inadequate remedies.

"The paper," says Lossing, " at its nominal value, was made a legal tender for all debts, and by this measure, which Washington deeply deplored, many creditors, both public and private, were defrauded, but no permanent relief could be afforded, for confidence was destroyed. As the articles furnished the army, like all others, rose to an enormous nominal value, Congress very injudiciously fixed a maximum price above which the articles to be purchased should not be received. The consequence was that at this stipulated rate none could be got; and the army would assuredly have perished, had not this absurd regulation been speedily rescinded." These issues continued to depreciate until eventually they became entirely valueless, and many of the officers and soldiers of the army were ruined, and themselves and their families were reduced to beggary.

BANKS.

THE word Bank is derived from the Italian word "banco," meaning a bench. The Jews, who were the first to follow the business of lending money, were accustomed to assemble in the market places in Italian towns, seated on benches, there to transact their business. The term "bankrupt" was first applied to those whose seats or benches were broken up or removed when they failed in business.

Banks are of three kinds: Banks of Deposit, Banks of Discount, and Banks of Circulation. The earliest establishment of the latter kind in Europe was founded near the close of the twelfth century, and was called the Bank of Venice. This was the earliest bank of circulation on the Continent. As a bank of deposit, however, it had had an existence for ten years previous to this time.

A plan of a National Bank was first proposed in this country by Robert Morris, of Pennsylvania, the distinguished financier and statesman, and was submitted to Congress on May 17th, 1781, and passed that body on the 26th of the same month. The bank commenced operation, with a capital of four hundred thousand dollars, in January following. In 1790, Alexander Hamilton, then Secretary of the Treasury, urged upon Congress the importance of establishing a United States Bank. Though violently opposed, this method was adopted in the following year, as the only feasible mode of restoring public credit, and of discharging the many foreign and domestic debts incurred by Congress, as well as the several States, in carrying on the War of the Revolution. The bank commenced operations with a capital of ten millions of dollars, divided into twenty-five thousand shares. The dividends of the bank did not at any time, during its existence of twenty years, exceed ten per cent. per annum. The application made in 1808 for a renewal of the charter was opposed, as had been the first attempts at incorporation. The application was unsuccessful, and in 1811 the bank was obliged to wind up its affairs.

On April 3d, 1816, a bill for a second Bank of the United States passed both Houses, was signed by the President, and became a law ; the charter extended to March 3d, 1836. The bank went into operation January 7th, 1817. On July 10th, 1832, the President refused to sign a bill rechartering the bank, and returned it with a message stating his objections.

At the expiration of the charter granted by the United States, March, 1836, it was immediately rechartered by the State of Pennsylvania. On October 9th, 1839, it suspended specie payment for a second time, and on February 4th following suspended entirely, leaving nothing to its stockholders, its entire capital having been sunk, spreading disaster throughout the country. From that time banks increased in all parts of the Union, until the breaking out of the rebellion, when, according to official reports, they numbered 1,562 ; since then no accurate report has been received from banks in the South. There are already nearly six hundred National Banks doing business under the general banking law of the United States, representing a capital of over 100,000,000 dollars.

ORIGIN OF THE BANK OF ENGLAND.

As late as the Restoration, every merchant of "Merrie England" kept a strong box in his own house. When an acceptance was presented to him he counted out the crowns or caroluses. Those were the halcyon days of thieves, when a burglar would not unfrequently be able, after a single night's work, to retire with a fortune; when highway robbery was a lucrative profession, and its adepts were styled "gentlemen of the road."

By the end of Charles the First's reign it was discovered that it was safer and more convenient to have agents to keep the cash of commercial houses. This new branch of business fell naturally into the hands of goldsmiths, who were accustomed to traffic largely in the precious metals, and who had vaults where masses of bullion could be kept secure from fire and robbers. It was at the shops of the goldsmiths of Lombard-street that all the payments in coin were made. Other traders gave and received nothing but paper. But the same reasons which led the community to gather their cash into fifty vaults instead of leaving it scattered among a thousand, soon led them to see that it would be still better to keep it in one instead of fifty.

In William the Third's time the matter was freely discussed, and in 1694 it took the definite shape of a plan for a National Bank. The idea first originated with Mr. William Patterson, a merchant of London. It was brought to the attention of the king, submitted to the Privy Council, and when the details were completed it was laid before Parliament. The bill became a law on April 25th, 1694, and the bank was open for business on January 1st, 1695. It gained popular favor less by argument than by its manifest convenience and utility. It lived, grew, and prospered, and England has lived, and grown, and prospered with it. The stability of the Bank of England is almost equal to that of the British Government. All that it has advanced to the Government must be lost before the creditors can sustain any considerable loss.

A VISIT TO THE BANK OF ENGLAND.

The traveller who neglects to call and see "The Old Lady of Threadneedle-street," as the Bank of England is familiarly called, denies himself a visit to the greatest of England's "lions."

As you approach the remarkable building in which the immense business of the Bank is carried on, you observe an edifice of no particular architectural beauty, possessing no imposing or marked grandeur, calculated to awe the observer; and yet as you stand before an institution that exerts more moral and political power than any sovereign in Europe, you feel yourself in the presence of more than regal majesty. You have a burning curiosity to penetrate into the interior of this mighty and mysterious building looming up before you, and to do so you must first obtain an order from the Governor of the Bank. On presenting your card of admission, you are admitted into a private room, where a messenger is ready to conduct you through the different apartments, which cover an area of eight acres of ground. There are no windows on the side of the building or toward the streets, each apartment being lighted from the roof or the enclosed area. The first apartment we enter is the vault where the Directors and Cashier are counting bags of gold, which men are pitching down to them from a store-room above. Each bag contains a thousand pounds sterling, fresh from the mint, never having been opened. We next enter a room where the notes of the bank, received the day before, are being examined. Each note is carefully compared with the entries in the books, checked, and then placed in boxes to be stored away. It will be remembered that the Bank of England never issues the same note a second time, and to meet this immense demand for notes so constantly used (which when returned are destroyed), the bank has its own paper-makers, its own printers, its own e gravers, all at work under the same roof. Even the machinery by which its work is done is made in the same building. It receives in the ordinary course of business upwards of eight hundred thousand pounds, or nearly four millions of dollars, daily in notes. These are put up in parcels according to their denominations, then securely boxed up, labelled with their denomination and date of reception, and placed in the vault, to remain for ten years.

If in the course of these ten years any dispute in business or litigation arises concerning the payment of any note, the bank is able to produce the identical bill. At the expiration of the ten years the notes are taken out and ground up in the mill, to be made into notes again.

Into the room where the bank-note paper is manufactured we are next led. The process of manufacture is carefully conducted. The paper is manufactured with the greatest care from the finest of linen rags. It passes off from the machines in narrow sheets, stamped on both sides with eccentric ruled or engraved plates in lines with letters expressing the denominations of the bills. The most beautiful and yet complicated operation in the whole bank is a register extending from the printing machinery in this room to the general banking office in another part of the building. This register marks every sheet of paper that is struck off from the press, and at the same time records it in the banking office, so that not a note can be manufactured by the persons employed, that is not recorded in this office.

A similar register or shaft passes through all parts of this immense building, touching at every apartment, and terminating in the general banking office. To this shaft are also attached sixteen clocks in different parts of the establishment, and the whole is regulated with such a nicety of precision that they never vary a second of time, and the whole sixteen strike the alarm the same moment.

In another room we find the weighers assorting the gold to detect the light coins. The machine is simple, and resembles the letter-weigher in common use. The coins are placed so as to slide one by one upon the spring scale; and if the piece of gold is of the standard weight, the scale rises to a certain height, and the piece slides off; if less than the standard weight, it rises a little higher, and the coin slides off on the other side. We may watch the operation of this machine for many minutes without discovering a coin under weight; and if we venture to ask what is the average number of light coins to a hundred or thousand of standard weight, we are politely informed by the messenger that that is a question which the weigher is not allowed to answer, and that he is not allowed to know the number himself.

We next enter the engravers' room, where are found more persons employed than in any other apartment. Some two thousand workmen, altogether, are employed in the building. The system of engraving seems to be almost perfect, the various parts of a note being engraved by different artists, each one making a speciality of his part, and therefore excelling in execution of his particular task. The last room entered is that in which the notes are deposited which are ready for use. Here some twenty persons are engaged, arranging and cording the stacks of money that surround us on every side; and here, in the presence of thirty million pounds sterling, or one hundred and fifty millions of dollars, we may perhaps form some idea of the magnitude of the business done, and the power this mass of money exerts over the entire civilized world.

If England is, as some one has sarcastically said, " but a nation of shopkeepers," its capacious " till," which we have thus been examining, affords the surest guarantee of their substantial wealth and commanding business importance.

THE DOLLAR MARK ($).

Much controversy has arisen as to the origin and meaning of
the peculiar mark used to denote dollars. Some have attributed
it to a corruption of the two letters U. S., used to represent
Federal currency, which afterward in the hurry of writing were
run into one, the U being first made and the S put over it. Some
writers say that it is derived from the contraction of the Spanish
word *pesos*, "dollars;" others from the Spanish *fentes*, "hard," to
distinguish silver from paper money. The more probable expla-
nation is, however, that it is a modification of the figure 8, having reference to eight reals, as the dollar was formerly called.

The word dollar itself is regarded as derived from the German
"Thaler."

WHAT CONSTITUTES A LEGAL TENDER.

This is regulated entirely by law. The Constitution of the
United States vests in Congress the exclusive power "to coin
money, regulate the value thereof, and of foreign coin." Nor
can any State enact any law which shall make anything
but gold and silver coin a tender in payment of debts. It is
proper to add, however, in this connection, that bank-notes are
considered as a sufficient tender, unless objection is specifically
made to them. The decisions of the Courts in the several States
are tending strongly in favor of regarding bank-notes, judicially
as well as commercially, as money.

Congress has fixed by law the respective sums for which coins
issued by it from its mint shall be received as a legal tender, as
also of the rates of foreign coins current in the United States.

The gold eagle is a legal tender for the payment of ten
dollars, the half eagle for five dollars, and the quarter eagle

for two and a half dollars. The double eagle is made a legal tender for twenty dollars. By the above is meant that gold coins are legal tender for the payment of all sums equal to or above their respective denominations.

The gold dollar is a legal tender for one dollar. The silver dollar, half dollar, quarter dollar, dime, and half dime, are declared to be legal tender in payments of debts for all sums not exceeding five dollars.

The three-cent piece is a legal tender in payment for all sums of thirty cents and under.

Copper coins are not recognized as money, and are not good as a legal tender for any sum.

NOTE.—At the present time the Greenback and National Currency are the only paper issues that are regarded as legal tenders in payment of debts.

AMERICAN BANK-NOTE COMPANY.

———•◦•———

In 1858, the following bank-note firms, nine in number, were consolidated under the name of the "American Bank-Note Company," and were duly incorporated as such: Rawdon, Wright, Hatch & Edson; Toppan, Carpenter & Co.; Danforth, Perkins & Co.; Bald, Cousland & Co.; Jocelyn, Draper, Welch & Co.; Wellstood, Hay & Whiting; New England Bank-Note Company; John E. Gravit; Edmands, Jones & Smillie.

By uniting the talent, skill, experience, and mechanical ingenuity of the above firms, their ability to execute whatever may be intrusted to them, both as to design and finish, cannot be questioned.

Since then, an association under the name of "National Bank-Note Company" has been formed for the same purpose, and, still later, another styled the "Continental Bank-Note Company," all located in New York city. Prior to 1862, all the money issued by the Government was executed by the bank-note engravers of New York; but now the enormous aggregate of the national currency, with the exception of the notes issued by the National Banks, which are engraved in New York, are engraved and printed in the United States Treasury buildings, under the super-intendence of the Treasury Department.

BANK-NOTES:

Their Counterfeits and Means of Prevention

Counterfeit Notes are those which are intended to be fac-similes of the genuine.

Spurious Notes are those which differ entirely from the genuine.

Altered Notes are those whose title, locality, or denomination has been extracted, and some other one pasted or printed in its place.

The term " raised note " is sometimes applied to those bills in which the actual denomination has been eaten or cut out, and in its place another and larger denomination put over or raised by a die: sometimes it is done by hand.

The increase of counterfeit, altered, and spurious bank-notes, during the last few years, and the immense losses sustained by the public in consequence of their general and constant circulation, demand that some measure of prevention should be adopted. The subject is daily acquiring a new interest.

It is well known that the country is inundated with spurious bank-bills, many of them beautifully executed. Some are *genuine bills* of broken banks, altered to represent those of good banks.

Some also are impressions from *genuine plates* of insolvent institutions, which are changed in the lettering, to bear a general resemblance to any bank in the country; and all genuine bills are more or less liable to be altered from low to high denominations.

The people of the United States lose in almost every form by paper money. The trade of the counterfeiter is now carried on to such an alarming extent, that the great number of counterfeits are regarded as the weightiest objection to a paper currency; and until the community become familiar with the characteristics of genuine bank-notes, and the characteristics of a genuine engraving, they cannot escape heavy losses and imposition from counterfeits.

2

A thorough knowledge of the manner of engraving bank-notes will render the detection of a spurious production a matter of certainty.

It is proposed in this work to familiarize the reader with the basis upon which all genuine bank-notes are constructed; * to give illustrations in counterfeit and genuine work, until, becoming thoroughly familiar with the principal points of each, he will obtain thereby an infallible key to the detection of all fraudulent issues.

It is remarkable, in a business community like ours, in which everything relating to profit is so perseveringly kept in view, that so important a feature as that of being able to distinguish a good bank-note from a bad one, should have received so little attention. It is evident, notwithstanding the large number of publications devoted to the description and detection of fraudulent issues, that the number of forgeries is increasing every day. It is also certain that those who consult and rely most upon the pages of these detectors, obtain nothing but vague and contradictory ideas, of no permanent value whatever, except to learn the various rates of discount that much of our banking currency is subject to, in certain localities; and who, after years of perplexing study, find themselves as ignorant of the subject of detecting counterfeit notes as when they first began their inquiries. Hence it is that so many persons have abandoned the idea of ever becoming competent judges.

A great point advanced by those who condemn the present mode of bank-note engraving is, that imitations, however crude and indistinct they may be, so long as they bear a general resemblance to genuine bank-notes, will and do deceive the generality of mankind. Now this is all very true, and only proves the position we maintain, that the business community must possess themselves of the necessary information that will enable them to

---

* The reader is referred to the article on "Making Money," from Harper's New Monthly Magazine, at the end of this Treatise.

discover and decide with unerring certainty the difference between genuine and counterfeit work. Now, the true method of detecting counterfeit bank-notes will be found, on careful examination, to be quite simple.

The method of instruction adopted in this treatise, is upon the principle that it is impossible to detect a counterfeit article, without an intimate knowledge of the genuine; and the ability to detect the one is in direct ratio to the knowledge possessed of the other.

The accompanying Bank-note Designs and Illustrations were prepared expressly for this work, and are of so general a character as to embody all the particulars that go to make up the genuine bank-note; and when the reader becomes thoroughly acquainted with these, he is in reality familiar with the entire bank-note issues of the country, as all genuine bank-note engraving is essentially the same, and the few distinguishing features are common to the entire bank-note currency.

BANK-NOTE PAPER.

One of the chief safeguards against counterfeits is in the manufacture of the paper on which the bills are intended to be printed.

The paper on which the notes of the Bank of England are printed is of the finest texture; being strong, it preserves its integrity, and as the bank never issues a bill a second time, they always present a new and clean appearance. Our banks reissue their bills as long as they will hold together. The latter are easily torn and mutilated, causing a loss and destruction of no small amount to the public, and correspondingly great profit to the banks.

GENUINE BANK-NOTE PAPER

Is always of a superior quality, possessing a fine, glossy surface a substantial body, and in its manufacture beauty and utility are combined.

THE COUNTERFEIT

Is of a light grayish color, soft to the touch, is generally fuzzy, is easily torn, and presents a finish very unlike the genuine.

ENGRAVING.

By the engraving is meant the lettering, scenery, and vignettes —commonly called pictures. A good bill is a pretty and perfect picture. All bank-note engraving executed at the present day is substantially alike; no difference can be discovered between any branch of it—whether engraved by one firm or another. The present system of bank-note engraving is acknowledged by brokers and bankers to be essentially perfect in every respect. A counterfeit has never yet been made which, on close examination, does not prove that the difference between a genuine and counterfeit bill is one which, if not always patent, is yet always easily discoverable. The whole face of a genuine bank note, under the present system of engraving, must be fine, even, and steel-like, every object represented perfectly clear and distinct, with uniformity in workmanship, color, etc.

The banks of this country act on the principle that the more expressive and elaborate the engraving is made to appear on the face of the bill, the less danger there is of its being counterfeited; and the Government have made counterfeiting upon their issues still more difficult by covering the backs of their bills with beautiful vignette and geometrical lathe-work.

COST OF BANK-NOTES.

The cost of engraving some of the showy notes of our banks, with beautiful vignettes, faces of bank presidents, Franklins, Washingtons, railroad cars, steamboats, ships, etc., is in many cases from five hundred to one thousand dollars, and some of the Government issues are still more expensive; for instance, the plate representing the landing of Columbus, seen on the back of the fives of the National Bank-notes now in circulation, cost not less than three thousand dollars, and that only covers the cost of engraving the plate for the back of the note, all of which is done to prevent them from being easily counterfeited.

The Bank of England, on the contrary, places no reliance whatever on fine and costly engravings. They print their notes with plates, the text of which might probably be executed for from forty to fifty dollars, and they have no counterfeits except those so clumsily executed as to deceive no one except the most ignorant; but their chief reliance is upon the manner of manufacturing the paper, and the geometrical lathe-work represented on the notes.

The eccentric ruling is executed on the plates by machinery, and the lines vary and diverge in so many ways, that after one set of plates are made and the tools destroyed, the bank itself cannot reproduce it, or make a fac-simile of the plate. It proceeds on the principle that what one man can engrave by hand, another can copy; but what one tool produces on a plate by eccentric ruling, operated on by machinery, no other tool can be made by the same machine to produce its exact fac-simile or counterfeit. The paper on which the notes are printed is, as we have before observed, of the finest quality, and constitutes no small item of expenditure in the "furniture" of a bank.

The engraved plates, the paper, and the printing, cost in the aggregate our American banks many thousands of dollars, this

amount varying with the expensiveness of the engraving, and the
extent of capital represented by the paper to be put in circulation.

GENUINE PLATES IN THE HANDS OF
COUNTERFEITERS.

Before proceeding to a detailed description of the several parts
of a bank-note, it may be proper to allude to the manner in
which counterfeiters have been successful in getting possession of
genuine plates.

There are quite a number of genuine dies now in the hands of
counterfeiters, which were obtained at a sheriff's sale of the
property and effects of Messrs. Durand & Co., who formerly did
an extensive business in bank-note engraving. The property of
Burton, Edmonds & Co. shared the same fate. These dies are
such as were then used by a number of banks ; and counterfeiters,
by combining them in different ways, succeed in giving to portions of bills the appearance of genuine.

Formerly it was a general practice with banks to purchase and
keep in their possession the dies of their bills; in transporting
the dies, however, from the engraver to the bank, they have in
several instances been stolen. With the genuine dies in his possession, the counterfeiter is of course enabled to produce a bill which
will, so far at least as the engraving is concerned, readily deceive.

At present it is the custom with the bank-note companies to
retain possession of the plates. Bank-note engravers may fail,
and even extraordinary diligence may not be sufficient to circum-
vent the thief; but it is believed that a careful attention to certain
rules, hereinafter given, with regard to the general execution not
less than the engraved dies, will be sufficient in all ordinary cases
of this nature to prevent imposition.

GEOMETRICAL LATHE-WORK.

The Geometrical Lathe is a very perfect and costly machine used by engravers for the purpose of producing very fine and beautiful circles or curvilinear figures. The work done by this machine may be seen principally on the counters and end-pieces of bank-notes, and on the backs of the greenbacks.

GENUINE.

In the genuine bank-note it will be found, on a close examination of the lines or circles produced by this machine, that they seem to radiate from a *common centre*, and are symmetrical and *uniform*. The circles or counters on which the figures representing the denominations of the notes are placed are made by the machine, and appear, on a close examination, beautifully interwoven and regular.

In a genuine note, such is the extreme exactness of the work done by these machines, that there is never in the lines or circles, whether concentric, eccentric, or geometric, the slightest possible irregularity or imperfection.

COUNTERFEIT.

In a counterfeit bill these lines and circles will be found, on close or even ordinary scrutiny, to be broken, blurred, and irregular—as in counterfeits the work is never perfect. In a genuine bill, as before observed, these circles on the face or back of the note seem interwoven—a network of circles, all perfect and seemingly starting from a *remote centre ;* in a counterfeit they have the appearance of a mere surface impression scratched on the bill, and an observer, on scrutinizing the portion of the note made up of such circles and lines, will seldom fail to distinguish between the genuine and false.

PARALLEL RULING.

The ruling engine is used by engravers for the purpose of making the parallel rulings on notes, as also for shading letters, skies, and figures.

Genuine.

In a genuine note, the characteristics of the lines made by this machine, in the hands of the engraver, are that the lines are exactly of the same size, are exactly parallel, and at regular distances apart throughout—they are fine, clear, and distinct. The same criticism is applicable to the shading done by this machine, although to a casual observer it seems as if done with a brush. When examined, it resolves itself into innumerable fine lines, each *perfect, regular*, and uniform, and presenting a smooth and finished appearance. A small magnifying glass will greatly assist the learner in examining shadings and other machine-work.

Counterfeit.

In stating the characteristics of the work done by this machine on a genuine bill, we may readily *divine* what is not and cannot be seen on a counterfeit.

The delicate and perfect shading of the genuine engraving cannot be successfully imitated; the unevenness of the lines, and the coarseness and scratchy appearance of the counterfeit, done by hand, is easily noticed. It is but necessary to call attention to the work, and the difference is readily perceived: *breaks* in the continuity, and variations in *thickness,* are the indications of the counterfeit in these particulars. See Plate 4.

MEDALLION RULING OR ENGRAVING.

Medallions are the raised patterns or heads generally seen on bank-notes. They are always copied from a medal or raised pattern, and hence the name.

GENUINE.

The distinguishing characteristics of this, as seen on a genuine note, are, that in heads or figures the perspective is perfect; the delicate shading, caused by the approaching and receding of the lines, gives a prominence to the representation. If it is a head, the profile has all the boldness of a medallion on a medal. The waving of the lines is distinct, perfect, and continuous, and the lines of which it is made up, when crossing each other, do so in the centre, and form perfect squares. To give an accurate profile requires elaborate care, such only as can be given by those who have made such work a life-study.

COUNTERFEIT.

The perfection to which line-engraving has been brought, in the representation of raised or bas-relief figures, makes counterfeiting, in this particular, easily detected. In a counterfeit note, the imperfections are seen in the faulty and flattened appearance of the figure.

If a head is represented, or attempted to be, either an unequal and unnatural prominence will be given to one part, while another part is sunken, or a stiff, unnatural appearance is given to the figure. The lines, delicate, beautiful, and complicated, in the genuine, which appear increasingly so when subjected to the more rigid scrutiny of the unaided eye, or whose beauties are more distinctly noticeable when examined through a magnifying glass, in the counterfeit appear increasingly disfigured, imperfect, and scratchy, and the face, if the representation is a head, is expressionless; cheeks are unnaturally prominent, or frequently graced with a spot in the centre, as if caused by broken lines.— See Plate 2.

VIGNETTES.

By vignettes is meant the ornamental figures or embellish- ments, as pictures, seen on a bank-note. The perfection to which the art of engraving has been brought is nowhere more clearly seen than in the beauty and elaborate finish of these vignettes.

We will pass in review some of the principal features of the more general figures and representations in use, and their more salient peculiarities.

PRINCIPAL FIGURES.

In all bank-notes there is some particular figure to which prominence is given.

In genuine notes, this figure will bear the closest scrutiny as to finish and symmetry, even to the minutest details.

COUNTERFEIT.

The principal figure on a counterfeit note may be equally prominent, but as it will probably be the best part of the engraving, it will serve, by the glaring disproportion between it and its surroundings, as to labor and general appearance, only the more clearly to indicate its true character. The general criticisms made as to a blurred and scratchy appearance of counterfeit notes are peculiarly applicable here.

PORTRAITS.

In no department of the counterfeiter's art has he met with more signal failure than in attempting to delineate the "human face divine," which, as some one has beautifully and truthfully observed, "is the painted stage and natural robing-room of the soul."

GENUINE.

In the true bill, the mouth, eyes, and face have an expression clear and distinct.

The hair, even in its most delicate wavings and strands, is accurately copied. The hands, and especially the fingers, will be found proportioned to the figure. The texture of the skin has not escaped attention, and indeed, in every respect, to the very minutiæ of detail, the portrait will bear close scrutiny.

The more familiar portraits, as those of Washington, Franklin, Clay, and Webster, "the old familiar faces," will strike the eye at once as being accurate, and the longer and more critically observed, the more perfect will the resemblance appear.

COUNTERFEIT.

In the counterfeit, the eye will be found not unfrequently without a pupil; the delicate lines about the mouth omitted or constrained so as to give a rigid and unnatural expression to that very important feature of the face; black lines encircle the head, spots and broken lines appear on the cheek and neck, none of which are seen on genuine notes. Bank-notes may be so nearly worn out, it is true, as to make it no easy task to trace and follow out the symmetry and fineness of all parts of the portrait; but if any portion of the portrait is left entire, our remarks will be found applicable to that portion.

MALE AND FEMALE FIGURES.

GENUINE.

The general characteristics noticed above, under other heads, are applicable here. The larger proportion of vignettes will be found to consist, it is believed, of female figures. The drapery here is particularly noticeable. It will be found to represent beautifully the folds and texture of different kinds of cloth, and, as it embraces the figure, will float and hang gracefully and naturally. Even the gloss of broadcloth, as in the garments of males, will be found transferred to the picture. In attention and fidelity to detail, a male or female figure, in a genuine bill, will have all the characteristics of the Pre-Raphaelite school of painting.

The male figure differs in no respect from the female, except, of course, that it is more masculine, and the dots and lines representing the flesh are closer to each other, and appear coarser; but the eyes, mouth, hands, feet, and general expression are determined in precisely the same manner. Indians have their dark complexion and muscular appearance; the white of the eye is clearly seen, and the fingers and toes are properly developed. See Plates 1 and 3.

FACES AND FIGURES IN DETAIL.

Before passing from the subject of portraits, and male and female figures, it will, perhaps, be serviceable, though at the expense of some repetition, to glance more particularly at the *details* of the figures. What we have said in the last two subdivisions under those heads, has reference to the " tout ensemble " of a bank-note rather than to particular portions of it.

1st, Hair.

Genuine.—The arrangement is neat and easy. If curled, as in the case of female heads, the ringlets will be *graceful* and *natural ;* on examination, the strands will be discernible, and the difference between the straight, black hair of the Indian, the close, curled hair of the negro, the flowing locks of a girl, or shaggy tufts of hair of a man, will distinctly appear. Look well to the texture of the hair. The reflection of the light upon it should be noticed.

Counterfeit.—The arrangement of the hair is very often clumsy. The great difference between the hair, as to texture and general appearance, noticed above, is not made apparent; it has a smoky, undefined, and indistinct appearance.

2d, Eyes.

Genuine.—The eyes on a genuine bank-note are the most expressive feature ; they give an individuality to the figure ; the white of the eye is clear, as in a good painting ; the eye will watch, and seem almost to speak to you, as you turn the picture from you. In examining them, it will be well to look at both at the same time, and the naturalness of their expression will then be manifest. See Plate 1.

Counterfeit.—More perfection has been attained by counterfeiters in representing the eye than any other feature of the human countenance. It is known that persons are apt to look first at the eyes of a picture, and hence the skill bestowed on this feature of the engraving. It is not exaggeration, however, to say that in more than half of the counterfeits, the eye is a mere dot, of course expressionless, and that almost *invariably* the shading around the eye is too dark, frequently black, giving a frowning expression. The eye is frequently too far *recessed* into the head, owing to defects of *shading*—too dark, black, and heavy. The distant one is most imperfect. Look directly at both pupils, and if either is crooked, which is often the case, it will be noticed.

3D, CHEEKS.

Genuine.—The shading gives a full, but natural prominence to the cheek; the high cheek-bone of the Indian is noticeable. The wrinkles of age, as well as the dimples and rounded lines of childhood, will appear according to the age of the person represented.

Counterfeit.—Here the cheeks appear sunken; the individuality noticed above does not appear; the shading done by hand is always imperfect, and if examined with particular reference to the prominence of the cheek, no one can be deceived.

4TH, NOSE, MOUTH, AND CHIN.

Genuine.—The nose should and does stand out from the face; the shading of the lines at the base of the nose enables us as it were to see *into* the nostrils, and, from its base to the top, the lines are so formed and shaded as to give it a natural—not too sharp or too flat, but a natural—appearance. The mouth is well formed, natural, and expressive; the lips are slightly pouting, the dimples are rounded naturally, and the chin is well thrown out. See Plate 1.

Counterfeit.—The nose seems to be lying on the face, instead of *standing out* from it; there is no particular prominence given to the nostrils, and the *shading* necessary to give them distinctness is wanting. The " isthmus " between the nose and the mouth is not represented. The mouth on counterfeit notes is almost without exception bad; it is either a slit on the lower part of the face, having no expression, or else too deeply *indented* at the sides, giving it there a black, unnatural appearance ; the curving of the lips is not seen, and character is wanting. Examine each separately, and then dwell for a moment on the combined expression of the eyes, nose, and mouth.

5TH, NECK.

Genuine.—The natural contour of the neck is displayed by the delicate shading, and its proportions perfectly harmonize with the rest of the figure. See Plate 1.

Counterfeit.—The neck is formed by coarse lines, which are intended to throw out the chin; but this, like all shading in counterfeit figures, will be detected from its smoky appearance.

6TH, ARMS, HANDS, AND FEET.

Genuine.—Passing from the head, we proceed to a critical notice of other parts. In a genuine note, the *arms* have given to them the curve and *plumpness* of nature; the muscles in the brawny arm of the smith will be prominent; the articulations of the elbow and wrist may be noticed; the arm will be so shaded as to give it the appearance of roundness; that is, we can seem to see it as if a natural arm was resting on the paper.

The same remarks are applicable to the hands and fingers; the joints and nails should be seen; the proportions of the hands to the body, and of the fingers to the hands, are just. The *position* of the hands is natural. If the hand is represented as upraised, the tension of the muscles will be seen. The feet are not often noticed, but the same general characteristics will be noticed here as in the hands; the toes should be *defined*, and the shading should represent them separate and distinct.

Counterfeit.—We might say here, summarily, that the characteristics of the feet, arms, and hands, on counterfeits, are their lack of symmetry; they are too flat. The rough lines of nature are smoothed over. The hands and fingers have no particular point;

the fingers are not separated, or if they are, they are *jointless*, with
out proportion and without life-likeness. The feet are seldom prominent; if bare, the toes are not distinguishable; in many cases the
little one is not formed; the nails are not seen; if represented en-
cased in boots or shoes, there will be noticed a lack of proportion;
sometimes the heel is not seen on both boots.

7TH, DRAPERY.

Genuine.—To represent the drapery of a female figure, requires
careful and assiduous application in the genuine bank-note; the characteristics of the drapery are easiness, adjusting itself naturally
and gracefully to the contour of the body. Folds of the cloth will
be shaded so as to look *like folds*, the buttons and button-holes on a
coat will be perfect, and, as in the case of a laborer, a careless,
easy, and yet perfectly natural appearance will be given to all
the garments.

Counterfeit.—The counterfeit note is seldom if ever successful
in any of these particulars. The dress, instead of appearing like
cloth, or some cotton, linen, or woollen substance, will look as if
made of *wire, depending unnaturally* from the body, and in a very
large number of cases which have passed under our observation,
we have found the minor details of dress, such as buttons, button-holes, loops, fringes, &c., &c., entirely wanting; the drapery
untidy and arranged in a slovenly manner; the dark material is of
a murky cast; and the delicate gossamer which enrobes the body
shows many very coarse threads.

LANDSCAPES.

Landscapes, farmyard scenes, domestic animals in the fore-
ground, railroad cars, ships and other representations of commerce,
constitute, next to actual portraits or imaginary figures, male or
female, the larger proportion of vignettes seen on bank-notes.

GENUINE.

In genuine bills, fidelity to nature is closely adhered to; a perfect bill will constitute as pleasing a study as a painting by a master in landscape, or the homelier representations of the *farm-yard* or the *horse-market*, as pictured by the brush of a Rosa Bonheur. New beauties will be revealed, and repay the closest attention. Regarded either in its entirety or in detail, the picture will be found finished and accurate. Trees and shrubs are neatly drawn, the limbs are well proportioned, and the foliage has a luxuriant appearance. The "still" water is represented by parallel lines, with streaks of white to show the reflection of light, and to produce a limpid effect. Clear skies are formed of fine parallel lines, and when clouds or heavy skies are required, they cross each other. See Plate 1.

COUNTERFEIT.

A perfect landscape, one which will justify rigid or prolonged observation, is never met with on the counterfeit bill. The landscapes look dark and forbidding, the trees appear as if blasted. The lines representing "still" water are scratchy rather than parallel, producing a muddy appearance. The sky is of the same consistency as the still water, and scarcely distinguishable from it.

DOMESTIC ANIMALS.

GENUINE.

Domestic animals of every description, horses, oxen, sheep, etc., are drawn to the life; their eyes, limbs, and proportions are perfectly accurate, and cannot fail to impress the reader favorably with the accuracy of bank-note engraving.

3

COUNTERFEIT.

Domestic animals are miserably executed; to see this, examine their eyes, limbs, and general proportions.

BIRDS.

GENUINE.

Great skill is displayed in engraving the eagle and other birds seen on bank-bills; the feathers are distinct and correctly defined, and will bear the closest scrutiny. See Plate 1.

COUNTERFEIT.

The counterfeit eagle is never well executed; the large feathers in the wings are represented by coarse lines running clear across the feather, instead of having the appearance of a quill running through the centre.

PERSPECTIVE.

GENUINE.

The perspective, showing a distant view of the surrounding country, is always clear and distinct; the sky fades away into distance until it mingles imperceptibly with the horizon.

The small figures in the background are always exceedingly well engraved. It is intended that everything placed there is for the purpose of being seen, and the outline and general character can always be recognized. See Plates 1 and 3.

COUNTERFEIT.

The perspective is always imperfect; the figures most distant are poorly executed, and will not bear close inspection, the general appearance being flat.

ARCHITECTURE, SHIPS, AND RAILROAD CARS.'

GENUINE

The lines denoting the surface of the materials in buildings are arranged with the law of light and shade; hence very fine lines, gradually becoming indistinct, leaving the surface white, denote the part upon which the light falls; and on the opposite or dark side, these are parallel and quite distinct. See Plate 1. Ships are well defined; the canvas has a clear texture; masts, spars, and tackling are correctly drawn. See Plate 3. Railroad cars are accurately delineated, and the most delicate parts of the machinery represented; wheels, valves and boilers, screw-heads and bolts can be seen. Smoke rises naturally from the engines, and is clearly defined.

COUNTERFEIT.

The architecture has a black appearance; and when it is represented in the distance, the lines, which ought to be quite fine, are coarse and heavy. Ships are poorly drawn; the texture of the canvas is very coarse, and the general appearance is bad.

Railroad cars are also poorly executed; the lines which denote the surface of the woodwork of which they are made, are heavy and indistinct; the car farthest from the eye is usually the most imperfect; and they always seem stationary rather than in motion.

LETTERING.

GENUINE.

The form and finish of the lettering on a genuine bank-note

are among the first things to attract the eye. The letters and figures will be found *clean*, the lines perfectly defined, the curves and hair-lines delicately and exquisitely executed. The round-hand or script-writing on a bill, that is, the " Pay to Bearer," etc., etc., is black, equal in size, and smooth throughout.

COUNTERFEIT.

In counterfeits the lettering is poorly executed, a hazy indistinctness blends with the shading of the letters, the roundhand writing is pinched and stiff, the outlines never have the *sharpness* of the genuine, the curves will be found to be *broken*, as if executed by an unsteady hand. The roundhand or script, "Will pay to bearer on demand," which is given in Plate 3, is to be found on all bank-notes, and must be carefully studied in the following manner : Fix your eye on the extreme point of the curve which forms the first stroke of the W, then trace with your eye slowly up the hair-strokes and down the heavy, until you have completed the letter. In the same manner trace all the letters, as it is the only method by which counterfeit work of this kind can be detected with facility. This should be practised frequently.

PRINTING.

GENUINE.

The most noteworthy feature of a genuine bill, aside from the engraving, is the artistic finish of the mere mechanical part of printing. The great care and attention with which all bank-notes are printed gives them a well-finished, legible, and distinct appearance. All parts of the engraving will be found to have received their proper quantity of ink, and every portion of every figure will be found neatly and fully developed.

COUNTERFEIT.

In consequence of the secret manner in which the " black art " of the counterfeiter is carried on, and the necessity to which he is subjected of doing by hand what machines do so much more perfectly for the engraver of genuine notes, the printing of the bill, even supposing him successful in getting a tolerable engraving, is poor. The character of the printing is one of the most palpable badges of a counterfeit note. The difference is so evident as hardly to escape the attention, when the observer's eye has been once directed to it.

INK.

GENUINE.

The characteristic of the black ink used by the engraver on genuine bank-notes is, that it is of a jet or glossy black when first applied, and retains its original appearance for a long time. The red letters are composed of a network of red lines, and are frequently used for lettering and devices on the back of the bill. Green is also used to a great extent upon Government issues. Blue is sometimes used, but not often. Engravers generally prepare their own ink.

COUNTERFEIT.

Partly owing to the printing, but attributable to a great extent to the ink used, counterfeit bills have a dull and spiritless appearance. The lines are indistinct, in a measure owing to the too quick absorption of the ink by the paper, and to its too easily *flowing*. The ink in a bad bill very soon fades, and the entire face of the bill becomes thereby confused and indistinct. When a counterfeit bill is new, the defects of the engraver are most readily noticed. When old—perhaps a "premature old age"—the deadness of the vignette is one of the surest proofs of its worthlessness. Notice carefully, and compare the color of the red lettering of the counterfeit with the genuine: the one will present a sharp, bright red appearance, and the other a dull, dark look. There is always a glaring contrast.

ENGRAVER'S IMPRINT.

On all genuine bank-notes the engraver's name can be found in small but distinct, neat, and perfectly legible letters. Great reliance may be placed on the appearance of the imprint. The letters, particularly the capitals, are perfectly executed, without the slightest flaw or imperfect turn in the entire name. The counterfeit bill either omits it altogether, or, in putting on the name of some responsible bank-note engraving establishment, does it in a manner so bungling and defective that a person of ordinary intelligence can hardly be deceived. The engraver's imprint is often not on a line, one name being much lower than the other; the letters, when examined separately, will be found imperfect, some of them being quite crooked; frequently some letters are left out. Similar defects might be referred to, but it is quite unnecessary; as the name of the establishment where the notes are engraved, being printed on the note, thus acts as an advertisement, and will be found to be one of the best executed parts on a genuine bank-note.

SIGNATURES.

GENUINE.

Any attempt to give an infallible test for determining the genuineness of a bank-note from the character of its signatures, would be of no practical utility. To persons accustomed to a particular signature, it may be a comparatively easy task to detect a forgery; not so, however, to others who are not experts. No reliance should be placed upon the handwriting alone. We may, however, state that there is a free, unconstrained, and easy character to genuine signatures, in which respect they differ very often from the counterfeit. On the counterfeit note the penmanship is generally of an inferior character, not unfrequently the signatures of both cashier and president appear to be in the same handwriting, and the "trail of the serpent" is seen in a forced, *cramped*, and unnatural chirography. As cases are not uncommon of bank presidents and cashiers as well as registers of bank-notes being deceived by imitations of their own signatures, it can hardly be expected that others may not be deceived also.

ALTERED BANK-NOTES.

WHERE the denomination is altered, or raised as it is sometimes termed, it is done by scraping or extracting with an acid the denomination, and a larger one printed or pasted in its place. The most dangerous of all notes are those altered from broken to solvent banks. This is usually done by extracting or dissolving by some chemical process the name of the State, the title of the bank, and the town or location of the same, and sometimes the signatures, and substituting others in their place. Sometimes the bank will be in the same State, and that will remain unaltered ; and sometimes the broken bank-notes of the same name or title are selected (for instance, banks with common names, as Commercial or Farmer's Bank, etc.) : in that case the State and town will be altered.

Bank notes altered from a smaller to a higher denomination can be easily detected by noticing the poor lettering, figures, lathe or relief work, and difference in the color of the ink, especially when held to the light. The denomination in the centre of the note, when examined letter by letter, will also disclose the fraud. If the " pasting process " has been resorted to, it can be detected at once by holding to the light. See Plate 4.

When the title or locality is altered, the note can be detected by carefully examining the letters and the parallel ruling which shades them. That portion of a broken bank-note where erasures have been made and other names substituted, always presents a bleached or faded appearance. The acid used to extract any portion of a bill destroys the texture of the paper, causing the ink to run when another name is printed in, giving it a blurred and dull appearance, and in every instance without the sharp finished outline of the genuine. All shadings, and sometimes letters, are composed entirely of parallel ruling, and the counterfeit can always be detected by the coarse and irregular thicknesses, and otherwise scratchy appearance, which it presents. By comparing the texture of the paper *between* the *letters* with that which is immediately *above* and *below*, a marked difference will be discovered both in appearance and color, caused by the action of the acid in making the erasure.

Wisconsin, Illinois, and, with few exceptions, all the banks of New York, are under a general banking law, and all the notes have the coat-of-arms, called the auditor's or comptroller's die.* This die will not be found on fraudulent banks or upon alterations from the broken banks, except where it is inserted from a counterfeit die. Sometimes the coat-of-arms of one State will be found upon the fraudulent note of another ; hence it is important that the student should familiarize himself with the coat-of-arms of the different States.

* Several other States have passed similar banking laws, but their banks have not so generally organized under that system.

PHOTOGRAPHED BILLS.

THE number of counterfeits produced in this manner is as yet not sufficiently great to demand special attention.

Many statements have been put forth by scientific men, respecting the danger of photography when applied to the counterfeiting of bank-notes, but fortunately it has thus far proved a failure. Some counterfeits by this system have been palmed off on the unwary, yet no judge of bank-notes need have any fear of being deceived. Bank-notes having lettering or devices on the back cannot be copied by this process. The parallel ruling, fine lathe-work, hair-lines, etc., etc., will be found very defective; the paper looks *greasy* and *transparent*, and feels oily. The impression seems to be on both sides of the bill, and is very *indistinct*, especially toward the ends, the centre of the bill being much darker than any other portion; the entire engraving presents a purplish or smoky appearance, frequently suggesting the idea that the note has been washed and the ink partially extracted.

FRACTIONAL CURRENCY.

THE same tests that apply to bank-notes in general are applicable to the fractional currency, as the engraving in the genuine is executed upon the same general and uniform principle by regular bank-note engravers. The counterfeits upon the early issue of this currency are easily detected by the inferior and indistinct geometrical lathe-work found upon the back, and by the difference in the color of ink used.

The more recent issue, with the portrait of Washington encircled by the *gilt oval*, is printed by what is called the "dry-printing process;" and the counterfeits are printed by the ordinary wet operation, which gives them, when compared with the genuine, a dark appearance; the gilt oval is dark; and by examining the parallel ruling, the lines will be found coarse, irregular, and broken, the lettering and engraving blurred and indistinct.

In order to offer greater facilities to those who desire proficiency in this acquirement, we have added (although at the expense of many repetitions) illustrations both in genuine and spurious work upon the same page, and would urge a careful comparison of the characteristics of these specimens. The aid of a magnifying glass is recommended in their examination.

GENUINE VIGNETTE AND PORTRAIT. Figs. 1 and 2.

Notice the regular appearance of the lines and dots, the well-formed eyes, nose, mouth, hands, and feet, and a perfect symmetry of beauty and finish.

Remarks.—This is the highest quality of engraving, and consequently the best security against counterfeiting. It requires many years of study and practice by a person of natural talents to master it; for these reasons few become eminent. Engravers of a high order of talent have never been counterfeiters; not an instance being on record, either in the history of the Bank of England or of banking in this country; therefore a counterfeit is always known by its inferior workmanship.

COUNTERFEIT VIGNETTE AND PORTRAIT. Figs. 3 and 4.

Notice the uneven and irregular appearance of the lines and dots, the badly formed eyes, nose, mouth, hands, and feet, and a general absence of beauty and finish.

Bank

One Dollar

Will pay

on demand

W. L. Ormsby. New York

Bank

Fifty Dollars

Will pay

on demand

W. L. Ormsby. New York

Remarks.—This vignette (No. 3) is inferior in workmanship, being the first attempt of an apprentice. Counterfeits are often better executed. The portrait, No. 4, is superior to the general run of counterfeits. The principal failure consists in the uneven dots in the face, the uneven background, and badly-formed eyes, nose, mouth, and hand. It requires a practice of three or four years to engrave even as well as this portrait; and it is doubtful if an engraver of such skill would, knowingly, prostitute his talents to a base purpose.

GENUINE GEOMETRICAL LATHE-WORK. Figs. 5 and 6.

Notice the perfect regularity of the white lines and black dots, or in some cases (Plate 2) of the black lines and white dots. Each row around the circle or oval must be perfectly uniform, being the work of a perfect machine, very difficult, if not impossible, for engravers to imitate by hand, so as to deceive a practised eye. To avoid alterations, *notice* that the work is perfect close to the figures and between every turn; and that there is an exact uniformity in the color of the ink, and general appearance of the workmanship; as sometimes the entire lathe-work is extracted, and a higher denomination reprinted. .

COUNTERFEIT GEOMETRICAL LATHE-WORK.

Notice the irregularity of the lines and dots in Fig. 8. The utmost skill of the hand cannot equal the machine. Low figures are sometimes scraped out, and higher added with a pen or small brush, as in Fig. 7. The work around the *outside*, in such cases, will be *genuine*, but *notice* the lathe-work close to and between the figures, and it will appear uneven and scratchy, like the example. The entire oval is sometimes extracted, and a higher denomination *reprinted.* It can be detected by a general appearance of incongruity, and also by examining the letters, or holding the bill to the light.

GENUINE MEDALLION RELIEF WORK.   Fig. 9.

Notice a regular set of lines running entirely across the medal. The variation from strict parallel ruling gives the shading, and forms the relief figure. The shade is dark where the lines approach each other; and light where they diverge. See that the work in and around the figures is perfect; that it has not been scraped, nor additions made with a pen.

COUNTERFEIT MEDALLION RELIEF WORK.

Notice irregularity in the lines, and failure in uniformity of shade. The hand always fails to copy machine-work so as to deceive an observing eye. Counterfeits are often better done than this, but familiarity with the genuine work enables any one to detect them. Guard against alterations, as in the preceding example.

GENUINE LETTERING.   Fig. 11.

Notice the shading of the letters in the word " Bank ; " it is done by a ruling machine: the lines are equidistant, and of a uniform shade. Notice in the writing perfection in the turns of hair-lines. For alterations, examine well the name of the bank, the State, the location, and particularly the words " One Dollar : " the genuine is always workmanlike, and not crowded. Examine the *imprint* of the engravers. It is always perfectly done in the genuine ; and a counterfeit can be detected by imperfections in this alone, when all other tests fail.

COUNTERFEIT LETTERING.   Fig. 12.

Notice the imperfect shading in the word " Bank ; " it is an attempt to imitate machine-work by hand. Notice the writing; it is imperfect in the "hair-lines." If the name of the bank, State, or location is altered, some bad workmanship will appear. The words "Fifty Dollars" are fair samples of alterations. The word "One" has been scraped out, leaving part of the O, and i-f-t-y added in a less workmanlike manner. The letter s, in the word "dollars," is in a crowded position, and is too large. The imprint is imperfect.

RECAPITULATION.

We have now given a series of rules which, if attentively studied, cannot fail to enable the reader to detect the frauds now so common in the issues of a counterfeit, spurious, and altered paper currency.

A glance at the ordinary counterfeits will frequently suffice to convince a person, who is acquainted with the requisites of a good engraving, and the manner in which it is done, of these frauds.

Others not so familiar, if the general appearance of the note is not so glaringly base as to indicate at once its character, will need to pass in review the several parts, and scan them critically in the following order :

First.—Examine the general framework of the note, the lettering, the title, the amount of the note, town, and signatures. Examine carefully all shadings, and make yourself thoroughly acquainted with the ink, printing, and paper of genuine notes.

Secondly.—Examine the counters, lathe and bas-relief work around them. Notice the bills that could be easily altered from a low to a high denomination. Hold to the light, or pass the bill briskly between your fingers, which will detect any pasting operation.

Third.—Examine the vignettes and portraits, carefully scrutinizing all points in detail, as before directed. The engraver's name will only detect spurious and counterfeit notes.

Spurious Notes are unlike the genuine: on some you will find genuine vignettes, lathe-work, and a part of the lettering. With few exceptions they are banks with common names, the lettering of the town and State poorly done. A part of them have no engraver's imprint. The printing, paper, and red lettering give them a suspicious cast:—can usually be detected by the engraver's name. With about a half dozen genuine vignettes, a few figures, lathe-work, and portraits, the scoundrels have made frauds upon twenty or thirty banks. Notice these dies, and refuse all notes that bear them.

Sometimes genuine plates from broken banks are obtained by counterfeiters, and altered by taking out the name of the bank, State, and town, by drilling, and inserting counterfeit names, by what is termed the plugging process. Notes printed from such plates can be detected by the poor lettering and shading of those parts, and by the paper and printing.

The reader is reminded of the fact that in most cases the vignettes and designs on bank-notes indicate the location of the banks (unfortunately this system is not properly adhered to); for instance, a view of the Falls of Niagara indicates an institution located in that section of the country; or the Bunker Hill Monument for a bank in Charlestown or Boston. Many altered and spurious notes can be detected by observing this rule. There are, at the

4

present time, many fraudulent notes in circulation, upon Eastern banks, bearing upon their face scenes representing negroes cultivating cotton, sugar mills, and many Southern plantation views; some with Western river-steamers, buffalo and wild-horse scenes; and various other absurd alterations, well calculated to deceive those who place no reliance upon their own ability to detect frauds of this character The scoundrels have even had the audacity to alter a bill of a broken Canada bank, with a vignette of the suspension bridge at Niagara Falls, and a portrait of Queen Victoria on right end, on left end a view of the Clifton House, and at the bottom the words "Incorporated by Act of Parliament," to the Waterbury Bank of Waterbury, Conn.   It seems hardly possible that a bill of this description could be passed upon any intelligent person, containing, as it does, so many points indicating that the bill originally belonged to Canada; yet many such bills find ready circulation with a large portion of the business community.

As yet the counterfeiters have not met with much success in their attempts to imitate the national greenback currency.   All imitations that have thus far appeared are so miserably executed that they cannot deceive any person who possesses even a shadow of knowledge as regards genuine engraving.   They are easily detected by the paper, printing, poor engraving, and by an entire failure to imitate the lathe-work, especially upon the back of the note.

In conclusion, it may be proper to say, that those who desire to become experts in this important study, must remember that "practice makes perfect," and that they not only should familiarize themselves with the rules and points laid down in this work, but that they must make frequent application of them in the examination of both genuine and spurious currency.   Those, however, who become interested, and are determined to improve themselves in this art, will soon acquire a fund of knowledge, the value of which cannot be overestimated, when we take into consideration the requirements of a *business education* in this advanced age.

ENTRANCE TO THE MERCHANTS' EXCHANGE, NEW YORK.

MAKING MONEY.

III.—THE AMERICAN BANK NOTE COMPANY.

THE " Bank Note Reporter" is a suggestive if not a very entertaining work, brim-full of facts. The lists of this financial *Index Expurgatorius* are headed with the significant warning, " Refuse the Notes of all Banks not found here," branding in a phrase a crowd of broken and fraudulent concerns. There are in the United States and the British Provinces, as we count, about 2000 banks whose notes are worth something—say from 20 to 100 cents on the dollar. Upon quite four-fifths of these fraudulent notes have been detected, usually several kinds upon each. Thus, of the 57 banks in the city of New York not one has escaped, the total number of fraudulent issues being about 350. The same ratio would give 12,000 for the whole country; but this is too large, since banks in the commercial parts of the country offer the greatest temptations to forgers. Still there are noted about 6000 different issues of spurious notes. Theoretically every man is liable to be defrauded by any one of these. At first view this would shake our confidence in the genuineness of any bank note. But the fact is, that in nineteen cases out of twenty a bad bill is detected almost as soon as its circulation is attempted. The number of "dangerous" counterfeits is very small. Not one person in a hundred has ever lost a dollar in this way.

For this almost complete immunity from loss we are indebted to the artistic and mechanical skill which is lavished upon our bank notes. This perfection has been attained by slow degrees. Nothing can be more rude than the Massachusetts notes issued in 1690, the first American paper money. Hardly better are the Continental Bills, first issued in 1775. These were engraved by Paul Revere, the best of the four engravers then in the country. A comparison of these with a United States Treasury Note of 1861 will show the progress of the art during the interval.

When our financial system began to assume its present form banks were multiplied, each of which demanded distinctive notes. Demand creates supply, and the best artistic talent in the country was attracted in this direction. At first a single artist engraved an entire plate, and not unfrequently printed it with his own hands. Afterward several combined to produce a plate, each doing that part of the work in which he excelled. Various machines were also invented, some of which, as Perkins's Transfer Press and Spencer's Geometric Lathe, contain the germs of the complicated instruments which, as we shall see, perform such an important part in producing a bank note of the present day. Subsequently private companies were organized, each containing artists excelling in some particular branch. Each of these companies produced excellent work, but as no one had all of the best talent, and as each had the exclusive control of some valuable mechanical invention, which the others could not use, no one note could combine all attainable perfection. Banks meanwhile demanded the most perfect notes that could be produced.

In 1858 the leading Bank Note firms, nine in number, united themselves into an Association, which was incorporated under the title of the "American Bank Note Company." The plates prepared by them are decidedly superior to any ever before executed. More recently another Association for the same purpose has been organized under the name of the "National Bank Note Company." The generous rivalry for artistic perfection between these two companies affords a sure guarantee that bank notes executed in America will continue to be, as they now are, superior to any others in the world. No other country has yet any thing to compare with them. The notes of the Bank of England and of the Bank of France are rude in comparison. Russia will soon have notes equal to our own, for the necessary plates are now in process of execution by the American Bank Note Company.

We propose to describe the various processes employed by this Company, and incidentally to give information which will aid in distinguishing a genuine from a spurious note. The operations of the Company are conducted in the noble "Merchants' Exchange" building in Wall Street, New York.

Passing through the fine portico, with its three ranges of pillars, each shaft, composed of a single piece of granite, 50 feet in height, and so large that three men clasping hands can hardly embrace it, we turn to the right, and enter the

CONTINENTAL BILLS.

MODELING AND DESIGNING ROOMS.

business office of the Company. This is by no means our first visit. Our present purpose is to revise our memoranda, so as to be sure that our entire account shall be strictly accurate. By a very necessary regulation no person can go through the establishment unless accompanied by some officer of the Company. On this visit we are, by appointment, to be guided by the President of the Company. We find him at the moment engaged in conversation with a couple of gentlemen. One of these we recognize, from published portraits, as Mr. Chase, the Secretary of the Treasury; the other is Mr. Cisco, the Assistant Treasurer in New York, whom we have met before in this series of papers. The Company, as we know, are performing a large amount of work for the Government, and the execution of the Demand and $7\frac{3}{10}$ per cent. Treasury Notes with the requisite speed has for months tasked to the uttermost all the facilities of their establishment.

Awaiting the disengagement of our escort, we pass up to the "Modeling and Designing Rooms," a handsome suit of apartments with a lofty

groined roof. The walls are covered with original drawings by Darley, Casilear, Edmonds, Herrick, and others. Port-folios filled with such drawings are opened for our inspection. A connoisseur in art could nowhere spend a more pleasant day than here. Some of the most curious of these drawings are those sent from Russia, which are to be reproduced on the Russian notes. These drawings have been used as designs for vignettes. They are made much larger than the engravings from them. A favorite size for the drawings for elaborate vignettes is about twice that of a page of this Magazine. When an engraving is to be made after one of these drawings, it is photographed in the exact size desired upon a plate of steel; the outlines are cut faintly upon the plate, which is then given to the engraver to fill up.

There are three general methods of producing pictures by engraving.

1. *Lithography.*—This is based on the chemical law that oil and water will not mix; or, as it is sometimes expressed, that "you can not wet grease or grease water." A drawing is

made, with pen or pencil, upon a kind of fine-grained porous stone. The pencil or the ink is of an oily composition. To print this drawing the stone is rubbed over with a moistened sponge; the water will not adhere to the lines of the drawing, but will to the parts of the stone not covered. Then a roller charged with an oily ink is passed over the stone; the ink adheres to the lines of the picture, but is thrown off by the moist portions. A sheet of paper is then laid on the stone, and a heavy roller passed over it. The ink is taken off by the paper, and a fac-simile of the drawing is produced. This process of wetting, inking, and rolling is repeated for every impression.

2. *Copper-plate Engraving.*—In this the lines and dots which make up the picture are cut, one by one, upon a plate of metal. To print from this, the whole plate is covered with ink, which also fills up the engraved lines and dots. This ink is carefully wiped off from the surface of the plate, leaving only that which fills the engraved lines. Then the paper is laid on the plate, which is passed under a heavy roller, which forces the surface of the sheet into the lines, taking up the ink. This process of inking, wiping, and rolling must be repeated for each impression.—Engraving on steel is precisely the same as on copper. Copper, being a soft metal, wears out rapidly in printing, so that but few perfect copies can be obtained from a copper-plate; steel, being much harder, furnishes a greater number of copies.

3. *Engraving on Wood.* This, in most respects, is the precise opposite of copper-plate engraving. A piece of box-wood is cut off across the grain. The surface is polished, and upon this the artist, with an ordinary lead pencil, makes a drawing, precisely as though he were making it on paper, giving every line, just as he wishes it to appear. This block is then given to the engraver, who cuts away every part of the wood not covered by the artist's lines; these are left standing in relief. The printing of a wood block is performed in the same manner as from types. The essential point of difference between copper-plates and wood-cuts is, that in the former the parts which appear are cut by the engraver; in the latter the parts which do not appear are cut away. To form an idea of the relative difficulties of the two processes, let any one, with a black pencil and white paper, try to make a copy, line for line, of any of our engravings. If he succeeds, he will do just what the copper-plate engraver might have done. Then let him try, upon a black slate with a white pencil, to make a perfect fac-simile of his other drawing. He must mark around all lines which he wishes to appear, leaving them black, and covering the interspaces with white. If he succeeds, he will have done just what the wood engraver has accomplished.—Wood engraving has within a few years been brought to a high degree of perfection. Without

THE DAY WATCHMAN.

GALLERIES AND ELEVATOR.

it no illustrated publication of large circulation could be produced, because it is the only means by which copies can be produced with the necessary rapidity. But there are certain effects within the reach of the copper-plate engraver quite beyond the reach of the engraver on wood or of the lithographer. These are just the things which are demanded in a bank note. Thus, the copies of the United States Treasury Notes, which will be found in this article, are engraved on wood

PICTORIAL ENGRAVING ROOM.

in the best manner possible. Let any one compare these with the notes themselves, and the difference will at once be apparent. Engraving upon copper or steel is the only style used for bank notes.

We shall have occasion, in following up our subject, to visit the Modeling Room again. At present we will accompany the President, who has joined us, on a tour through the establishment. We follow a passage, and ascend a half flight of stairs, where we find ourselves confronted by the day watchman. We note, here as elsewhere, the massive construction of the building. The floors and stairs are composed of massive blocks of granite; the walls are of solid stone or brick; the railings are of iron. From this point passages and stairways diverge to the various working rooms, and no person unless an employé can pass without a special order from the heads of the Company. The employés even can only go to their own department. engravers taking one way and printers another. A man may have been for years employed in one department without ever having visited the others.

We ascend first to the Pictorial Engraving Room. Here the steel-plate, with the drawing photographed upon it, is placed in the hands of the engraver, who proceeds to fill out the outline. The position, shape, and size of every line and point must be carefully considered; these are cut, one by one, in the hard metal. Sometimes a single person executes the whole of a vignette; but more frequently several are suc-

cessively employed upon it, one engraving the figures, another the landscape, another the animals, and so on, each performing the part in which he excels. From one to four months' constant work is required to produce a single portrait or vignette. This plate, which is called a die, is not used directly for printing, but as a mould, so to speak, from which perfect copies are made upon the note-plate, by a process which we shall presently see.

First, however, we must pass to the Lathe Room, where certain parts of a note are executed by machinery, with a delicacy and precision altogether unattainable by the human eye or hand. These we may designate by the general name of "checks." A check, with large letters or figures denoting the denomination of the note, is usually placed in one or more corners of the note. These are technically called "counters."

Some of this machine work is executed by the "Cycloidal Engine." The principle of its operation may be readily understood. A graver is arranged so as to cut a circle upon a plate fixed beneath it. Now while the graver is revolving, let a forward movement be given to the plate, and the line cut by the graver will assume a form like this, which is called a "cycloidal line," and may be described as that line produced by a point revolving about a moving centre. The particular curve will depend upon the relative velocities of

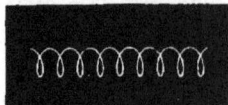

the two motions—the circular one of the graver, and the forward one of the plate. Thus, if the latter is comparatively slow, the cycloid will take this shape; if still slower, the curves will cross each other, instead of nearly touching. If the motion of the plate is comparatively rapid, the cycloid will take this form, or one still more open. Instead of a straight motion, a circular one may be given to the plate, in which case the line will follow the circumference of the circle. A succession of cycloidal lines, cutting each other, is sometimes printed over the whole, or a part of the face or back of a note. If, instead of a circular motion, an elliptical one is given to the graver, the figure will assume a quite different form, as in this example, which consists of two irregular cycloidal lines, cutting each other. The effect, however, is not pleasing, wanting that regularity of appearance which is the great security of machine work, as distinguished from that produced by hand. The Ruling Machine, which produces parallel lines far more accurately than can be done by hand, and the Medallion Machine, which, by a series of lines, gives the effect of a medal, are also used upon bank notes; but their work does not at present form a distinguishing feature.

Machine work, especially on a small scale, of a far more intricate character is produced by the "Geometrical Lathe." We will endeavor to explain the theory of this machine. Let a graver be so fixed as to cut a single curve of a waved line upon a stationary plate. Then let the plate be moved forward, and a continuous waved line, like this, will be produced; this curve may be made of any size or shape which is desired. Now, parallel with this line, let another of different pattern be cut over it, and the two will cross and re-cross each other in this manner. A third, and fourth, or any number of additional waves may be added, each additional one varying and complicating the general pattern. If the waves bear a regular relation to each other, the interstices will present a regular succession of forms. Now, instead of a forward motion, let the plate have a circular one, and these lines will all describe a waved circle. By means of "cams" and "eccentrics," instead of a circular motion, an elliptic or any curved motion may be given to the plate. Here is a skeleton check, showing some of the forms which may be given to a single waved line. Any conceivable form—an oval or square, an oblong or shield, a rosette or shell, may in like manner be produced. The following diagram shows at one view some of the effects of which the lathe is capable. The smaller central figure is a star, outside of this is a circle, beyond this a rosette with sharp points, and outside of all an altogether different rosette, with a curved outline. These diagrams have all been engraved for us by the machine itself. They have been purposely made much more simple than the checks actually used on bank notes, in order that the general form may be more readily distinguished. Any one with a glass and a sharp needle may follow the lines which compose these figures.

One additional thing must be noted. We said in a former paragraph that in a steel-plate engraving the line cut by the graver is black when printed. In our diagrams, as well as on the notes themselves, the line is white, the enterspaces being black. The reverse would be the case if these checks were printed from the dies themselves, or from a copy taken in the ordinary manner by the transfer press. This reversal—making that sunk on the plate which is raised on the original die, and vice versa—is effected by a process which we will not describe. Its effect, however, is evident. We may suppose, for instance, that a very careful engraver might possibly cut upon a plate a tolerable imitation of the white lines forming the figure in our last diagram. But what eye or hand could cut the black interspaces, and leave the white lines so regular and uniform? Yet this is just what the engraver must do who would reproduce on steel this figure; yet, we repeat, this is far less elaborate than those actually used on bank notes.

The United States Five Dollar Demand Notes, which are now familiar to most persons, present some good examples of lathe-work, which may be profitably studied. The counter in the right upper corner presents an oval with a waved outline, inside of which are successive patterns. The green checks in the centre are oblong, filled up with a wholly different pattern. The two large counters on the back are still different: while the small ovals which cover the greater part of the back consist of a border of delicate white lines crossing each other, within which is a green oval line, then a white one, then a solid

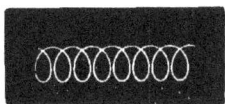

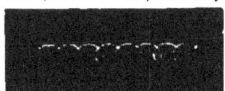

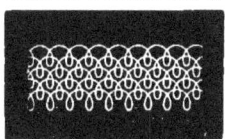

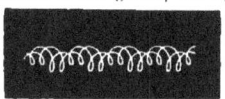

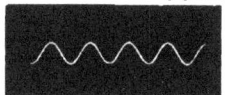

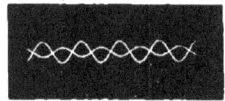

LATHE ROOM.

green centre, containing a "5" in white, all within a space not as large as a grain of coffee. By the aid of a glass every one of the lines whose crossings and recrossings constitute the pattern may be distinctly made out. The graver which has cut each of them in hard steel has passed many times over each, for at one stroke it will not cut sufficiently deep. At each passage it cuts about $\frac{1}{3100}$ part of an inch; about twenty cuttings are required to give the line its required depth. The machine must work with mathematical precision. A deviation of the half of a hair's breadth would destroy the whole work.

The "Geometrical Lathe" which produces this work is perhaps the most ingenious piece of machinery ever invented. Its general principles are, of course, familiar to all educated machinists. It is the combination of all of them so as to work together with unfail-

ing accuracy which constitutes the marvel. We have watched it for hours, and at each moment have found something new in its working, when explained to us by its skillful operator; for after all the machine itself, to produce the required effect, must be under the direction of human intelligence. It will do the work which is set for it with unfailing precision, but its work must be laid out for it. The turn of a screw, the substitution of one wheel for another, with the variation of a single cog, the shifting of the axis of an eccentric, will produce an entirely new effect; it may give distortion where perfect regularity is demanded. This lathe was built by the Company at a cost of more than ten thousand dol-

HARDENING ROOM.

lars, three years having been employed in its construction. It is the only one in existence, and its counterpart is, of course, wholly beyond the reach of counterfeiters; and yet, without it we can not see how they can successfully imitate its work. Notwithstanding its multifarious movements and complicated parts, its bearings are so accurate, that it is moved by the foot of the operator pressing upon a treadle, with the exertion of less force than is required to work an ordinary sewing machine. We have dwelt at length on this machine and its work, because we consider it a most important security against counterfeits; not exceeded in value even by the artistic perfection of the vignettes, portraits, and lettering.

The machine work of the die having been performed, the letters and figures appearing upon it are engraved by hand, and the finished "check" or "counter" is ready to be transferred to the bank-plate.

These dies, whether engraved by hand or by machinery, are made upon softened steel. They are hardened by placing them in crucibles which are filled up with animal carbon, hermetically closed, and placed in a furnace. The carbon, volatilized by the intense heat, combines with the steel, making it as hard as the finest razor-blade. They are then brought to the Transfer Room, and by means of a powerful press a roller of softened steel is passed over them. The pressure is regulated by the foot of the workman acting upon a system of compound levers. In the largest machine he can give a pressure of 35 tons. Under this pressure the softened roller is made to revolve over the hardened die, and receives the impress of every line. This rolling must be repeated over and over, in order to make the impression of the required depth. The machine must therefore work with perfect accuracy, each line falling at every revolution in precisely the same place. The roller is then hardened; and when the particular design impressed upon it is wanted for a bank note, it is in the same manner passed over the plate, which thus receives a perfect copy of the original die.

These rollers are in a sort the types from which a portion of a bank note is "set up." The selection and arrangement of them for any particular bank belongs to the Modeling Department. When a person wishes a note or series of notes prepared, he must first show that the bank is legally established, and that he is authorized to procure its plates. Without this precaution the Company will not undertake the work. In designing a note there are several points to be considered. The various denominations must all be different in appearance, and none of them must resemble any note of any other bank. Each must combine the various kinds of work adopted as securities against frauds, and must, moreover, present a handsome appearance. Then a bank frequently wishes its notes to have some special adaptation to its title or location. A "Farmer's Bank" will naturally wish an agricultural scene to appear on its notes; a "Merchant's Bank" will wish a commercial; an "Artisan's Bank" a mechanical scene; and so on. Then there will be prepossessions in respect to portraits. If the directors are Demo-

TRANSFER ROOM.

crats, they will probably wish Jefferson or Jackson, Douglas or Wright; if Republicans, Lincoln or Seward, Scott or Chase. An Eastern bank will likely wish Webster, a Western one Clay, a Southern one Calhoun. The agent examines the port-folios containing proofs of the dies in the possession of the Company. He has ample scope for choice, for there are some 20,000 of them. Of these probably 5000 are vignettes, 5000 portraits and emblematical figures, and 10,000 checks and counters. Aided by the officers of the Company, who take care that in combination and arrangement the notes of each bank shall be easily distinguishable from those of any other, this part of the plate is agreed upon.

Then, the general style and arrangement of the lettering is settled, and a sketch of the note is made. The vignettes, portraits, checks, and counters are now put upon the plate in their proper places by the transferring machine, and the plate is passed to the Letter Engraving Room, where the lettering is performed by hand. Here also is room for the display of artistic talent, for a good and bad lettered line differ almost as much as a good and a bad vignette or portrait. The Lettering Room employs a much larger number of artists than the Pictorial Room, because the lettering of each note must be to a great extent peculiar to it, while vignettes or portraits may be used, in different combina-

LETTER ENGRAVING ROOM.

tions, upon any one of a thousand. Here also the principle of division of labor comes in. One man's forte is German text; that of another is ornamental letters; that of a third is script. Each executes that part in which he excels, and the combined result of their skill appears on every note.

Our plate is now finished: the main one, that is, which is to be printed in black; for most bank notes now have the back and a part of the face in colors, for which separate plates are used. This complicates the process, and renders the work of the counterfeiter more difficult. But its special object is to afford security against photographic imitations.

At one time it seemed that photography and kindred arts would destroy every guarantee against counterfeit notes. Give the photographer a camera, a few dollars' worth of chemicals, and a quire of paper, and he could produce fac-similes of any note without limit. No matter how perfect the engraving, or how elaborate the machine work, he could in a few minutes make a copy exact to the minutest point. Science was invoked to remedy the evil which it had occasioned. Now photography can not, as far as we know, reproduce colors. Red, yellow, blue, and green, act like black upon the photographic plate. A red-haired man, for example, when photographed, wears a head of unimpeachable raven hue; the yellow of a footman's gorgeous plushes appears black in his photographic picture. So parts of bank notes were printed in red, blue, yellow, or green. These parts when photographed appeared black, as well as the part which were so in the genuine notes. But unfortunately all the colored inks in use were of such a nature that they could be discharged, with more or less facility, without disturbing the black ink. The counterfeiter would remove these colors, photograph the remainder of the note, and then print in the proper colors an imitation of the colored parts. An additional process was thus rendered necessary for the manufacture of a photographic counterfeit, but this was an easy one, and the labor was more than repaid by the security which was supposed to be given to any note printed in colors.

The production of an indestructible colored ink thus became a desideratum. This has been held impossible. Absolutely it is probably so. We presume no ink can be devised which may not be removed by chemical or mechanical means, or by a combination of both. Thus the coloring matter of the black ink used by printers is carbon finely pulverized. Put this dry upon paper, and it may be brushed off with a feather; mix it with water; and when the liquid evaporates the powder can be rubbed off. In printer's ink the carbon is mixed with oil, which binds it to the surface of the paper. Now an alkali combined with oil produces soap, which can be washed away. Let a piece of printed matter be saturated with alkali; wash it carefully with water and the oil disappears, leaving the carbon free. The problem, however, was to produce a

colored ink, not indeed absolutely indestructible, but one which could not be removed from a part of the note without, at the same time, discharging the black ink of the remainder. Even this was pronounced impossible. "The New American Cyclopædia" says: "No tint has yet been discovered which may not be chemically removed from the paper."

This important desideratum has, we believe, been attained in the "Green Ink," for the use of which the American Bank Note Company holds the exclusive patent. Four years ago it was submitted to the examination of the most eminent chemists. Among these were Messrs. Hunt of Montreal, Gibbs of the New York Free Academy, Torrey of the Assay Office, Horsford of Harvard, Silliman of Yale, Henry and Hilgard of the Smithsonian Institute. The composition of the ink was explained to them, and they were requested to apply to it the most searching tests known to chemistry, with such new ones as they could devise. They all replied, in substance, that they knew of no chemical means by which the green ink could be destroyed without, at the same time, destroying the texture of the paper on which it was printed; and it could be removed mechanically only by means which would, at the same time, remove the black carbon ink combined with it on the same note. Most of these eminent chemists have recently been asked whether in the interim any new discovery has been made which would lead them to change their former opinion. They all reply in the negative. We may therefore assume that the green ink which appears so largely upon the Bank Notes and United States Treasury Notes prepared by this Company, affords a perfect security against photographic counterfeits. The public must learn just what parts should be in green. If they do not in any bill appear of that color, or if they do appear in any other, the note may be assumed to be a photographic counterfeit.

The finished plates are now deposited in the Plate Room, from which they can only be re-

NIGHT WATCHMAN.

PLATE ROOM.

moved when actually wanted for printing, and never except by a written order from the Secretary of the Company. The importance of this room is shown by the care taken for its security. It is in the fourth story of the building, and can be approached only by narrow passages communicating with those leading to the various departments. At night these are patrolled by armed watchmen, who have duplicate keys to every room except this. Just before the door, and at the point where the passages converge, is the room of the Janitor, a gray-headed, jolly Hibernian, who seems to be always at his post. Through the half-opened door of his den we catch sight of a formidable brace of blunderbusses, a discharge from which would effectually sweep the narrow passages. He points out to us also a series of cunningly devised "peep-holes," as he calls them, through which he can watch every thing going on without himself being seen. Long habit has made him so watchful that he can not sleep comfortably without getting up half a dozen times in the night to take a peep through these holes to assure himself that all is right, and that the watchmen are duly performing their rounds.

The entrance to the Plate Room is secured by double doors of "chilled iron," with burglar-proof locks. These doors are never unlocked for a moment unless the keeper is within. Entering, the room looks like the casement of a fortress. Walls, roof, and floor are all of solid granite. The two windows, which look out upon the street, sixty feet below, appear like embrasures, showing the massive structure of the edifice. All around the room are cases with numbered compartments, in which the plates are deposited. An alphabetical register, comprised in several mercantile-looking volumes, tells the place in which every plate is deposited, so that it can be found at a minute's notice. Here are stored away plates for the entire issue of more than fifteen hundred banks in the United States: those for the Treasury Bonds of the United States and the Government of Canada; for the National Bank of Greece; for banks in Costa Rica, Guayaquil, Panama, and St. Thomas; for Swiss Railroad Bonds, and Postage Stamps of the British Provinces; besides those for Bonds, Drafts, Certificates, Bills of Exchange, and other Commercial Paper. In all, there are about 8000 plates deposited here. The falling of any one of these into improper hands would involve serious loss to the community. Well may every precaution be employed for the security of this room. It is really a "safe," more secure than any which we have seen, unless, perhaps, that in which the Assay Office keeps its bars and cheeses.

Passing onward, we glance into the Paper Wareroom, where a large stock is always kept in store. This is of no small importance; for the quality of the paper is one of the points to be considered in judging of the genuineness of a bank note. In the English notes this is the principal security, the engraving being of less importance. With us the quality of the paper is of less account. Still, as the paper used for bank notes is of a peculiar character, made for this special purpose, by only a few manufactories, it is essential that it should be closely watched.

PAPER WAREROOM.

Not a sheet can leave this room without being accounted for.

We now pass to the Counting and Packing

COUNTING AND PACKING ROOM.

Room, where a variety of operations are performed. Here the work is given out to the printers. Each man in the morning receives the plate which he is to print, and the necessary paper. These are charged to him. At night, when he has finished his day's work, he brings back the plate with his printed sheets, which are credited to him on the books. Here also the printed sheets are dried, pressed, counted, and sealed up for delivery to the persons authorized to receive them.

We now ascend a flight of stairs, and reach the Printing Room. This room, or rather series of rooms, present a busy aspect. They occupy three sides of a hollow square, of which the Rotunda of the Exchange forms the centre. Our illustration shows only a half of one of these three divisions. Turning around, a similar scene is presented to the view, which will be repeated at each of the three sides of the square. Rows of presses are ranged through each division. On some are being worked the black plates of a note; on others the green backs and checks; on others the red patterns which appear on various parts of the notes. According to our count there are in this room about 100 presses, giving employment to nearly 200 persons. The necessity for this large force will appear when we remember that each note, as now produced, requires at least three separate printings: First the black,

PRINTING ROOM.

Bank notes were formerly numbered with a pen. The numbers are now usually printed in red, by means of a very ingenious little press, so arranged that the action by which one number is printed changes the type for the next impression to the number immediately succeeding, without any possibility of error. Thus, if 666 has been printed on a note, the figures for 667 are presented for the next. The machines are arranged to present any number up to 7 figures. That is, they will give any number from 1 to 999,999. No two notes of the same "letter" can have the same number; so that a record of the "letter" and "number" is sufficient to identify any note numbered by the machine.

Not only are skillful workmen and accurate machinery requisite for the mechanical perfection of a bank note, but all the materials used must be of the best quality. Much depends upon the ink. This is all made by the Company, of much finer materials and more carefully prepared than is requisite for ordinary purposes. For black ink a carbon of the purest quality and deepest color is required. Formerly that made by burning the refuse of the wine-press was considered superior to any other. Now, however, an article quite as good is made from sugar. This is calcined in an air-tight iron vessel, and the result is a powder of intense blackness, capable of the most minute pulverization. It is carbon almost absolutely pure; chemically, as far as science can detect, this black powder is identical with the diamond. The black figures "500" on a bank note, which one gives for a diamond, by our most accurate analysis, differ nothing from that of the precious stone which is received in exchange.

In a small room we find a machine, for the invention of which almost every one has daily cause to be thankful. It is used to perforate those little holes in a sheet of postage stamps which enable us to separate them so readily. It consists of a couple of cylinders revolving to-

NUMBERING PRESS.

secondly the green upon the face, and third the green check upon the back. A fourth printing, usually red, is frequently added upon some part. Notes also wear out more rapidly than is generally supposed. A curious table, compiled from the records of the New York Banking Department, has been prepared by Mr. Gavit, showing that the average "life of a bank note" is about three years. That is, taking one with another, notes in three years become so worn and defaced as not to be fit for circulation. When such a note comes back to the bank it is destroyed, and is replaced by a new one. This period might be shortened with advantage to the public. The Bank of England never re-issues a note. If one was paid out yesterday, and comes back to-day as fresh as when issued, it is put away to be destroyed. We can not see the necessity of this; but we think a bank should never re-issue a note which has become at all indistinct.

A portion of the colored work of a note is printed from raised plates, like type, upon the ordinary hand-press. But the greater part of the printing is "copper-plate." The plate is laid on a brazier containing fire, for it must be warm to keep the ink in a sufficiently fluid state. The ink is applied with a roller all over the plate. The workman gives it two or three dextrous wipes with a cloth, and one or two more with his bare hand, removing all the ink except that which fills up the lines of the engraving; then places it on the press, lays the sheet of paper upon it, and by turning a winch passes it under the roller, which gives the impression. The whole operation is one of great nicety, for if the plate were not wiped perfectly clean the whole note would be blurred over; the paper also must be laid on in exactly the proper place, otherwise, when the colored pattern is added, it will not fall exactly in its right position. The presses must therefore all be of the most accurate description.

INK MILL.

PERFORATING MACHINE.

pumps water, moves the elevator, works the hydraulic presses, turns the ink mills, heats the building, and makes itself generally useful in a variety of ways. As may be readily conceived, in so large an establishment savings small in detail amount to large sums in the aggregate. Thus, the cloths with which the plates are wiped formerly consisted of rags from the paper-mill. But the supply from this source adapted to the purpose has of late fallen short of the demand, and it has been found necessary to have a fabric made for this special purpose. It is thin and soft, costing about six cents a yard. Formerly these cloths, when saturated with ink, were burned up; but as each printer will use about six cloths containing a yard each in a day, the entire cost for 100 amounted to a large sum. We saw a single bill of $2500 for this cloth paid by the Company. Now these cloths are all washed out by the steam-engine, and are used over and over until worn out. Then of the ink laid upon the plate, more than three-fourths is wiped off by these cloths. Now this ink is costly. The powder, for instance, which forms the basis of the green ink, costs a dollar a pound; that for the best black ink, costs not less than 50 cents a pound. This was all wasted when the cloths were destroyed. Now the green pigment is separated from the water in which the cloths are washed, and again made into ink, to be again wiped off and again recovered. The saving from absolute waste of cloths and ink can not amount to less than $5000 a year. This saving ultimately accrues to the public; for it enables the Company to do their work so much cheaper. If so much wiping cloth and so much ink are wasted in printing a note, its cost must be charged indirectly to the purchaser. This purchaser is immediately the bank, but ultimately every man who has occasion to use a note.

gether. The upper one is studded over with little punches which fit into holes in the lower one. A sheet of stamps—already gummed, dried, and pressed—is passed between these cylinders, and each punch cuts out a piece; the lower cylinder being hollow these pieces fall into it, and do not clog the punches. A hundred stamps are usually printed on a sheet, and 250 of these sheets can be perforated in an hour. Simple as this machine is, no one hit upon it for years after the introduction of stamps. A statistician might make a curious estimate of the number of years of human life that would otherwise have been expended in searching for knives and scissors, and then cutting stamps apart, which have been saved by this machine. Thus: It took so many seconds to cut off a stamp; so many hundreds of millions have been used; multiply these figures together, and reduce the product to years or centuries, and we have the saving. The cylinders are made in sections, like a row of wheels, so that the points may be adjusted for stamps of any size.

In all the American Bank Note Company employs about 350 persons, of whom more than 100 are females. There are about 60 artists and engravers: 250 are employed in the Printing and Counting Rooms; the remainder being superintendents and clerks in the various departments. As we have seen, the presses and lathes are all worked by human power. Still there is employment for a steam-engine of 20-horse power. It

ENGINE ROOM.

This and the following pages contain representations of one of the United States "Demand Notes," and of one of the 7 3-10 per cent. notes. They are not intended as perfect fac-similes. No attempt has been made to present the lathe-work checks and counters, beyond indicating their position and general figure. The parts which in the notes themselves are printed in green, are mentioned in the brief descriptions which are given of each denomination. The backs of all the notes are printed in green. They consist of elaborate combinations of lathe-work, different entirely for each denomination, each containing the letters and figures which show the value, repeated many times. No one who observes this, and notes the brief descriptions of the character and position of the different parts of the notes, will ever be defrauded by an altered Treasury Note.

UNITED STATES TEN DOLLAR DEMAND NOTE.

5. No Vignette. Crawford's statue of America on left end. "United States" at top in Old English letters. In centre, large "5" in green between two oblong checks, with "Five Dollars" in black across them. Counter in right upper corner, in black. Portrait of Hamilton in right lower corner.

10. Vignette, American Eagle. Portrait of Lincoln in left upper corner. On right end, Art, with palette and tablet. "United States" in square letters below eagle; under this, check, in green. Counters, with "10" on each side of Vignette.

20. Vignette, Liberty, with sword and shield. On each end oblong check, in green. Centre, black, with "20." Green checks on each side of Vignette.

(The Treasury Notes are signed, by different clerks, "For the Register of the Treasury" and "For the Treasurer of the United States." The places of the signature are indicated in our representation.)

50. Vignette, American Eagle on Rock. Corners, black, with "50," below Vignette "50" between two oblong checks in green. "50" and "L" repeated many times around margin.

100. Vignette, Portrait of Scott. Corners, upper corners, black, with "C," lower corners, green, with "100." Large ornamental "C," in green, on each side of Vignette.

500. Vignette, Portrait of Washington. Corners, black, with "500." Left end, Justice, with sword and scales, seated on chest. Right end, Ceres, with cornucopia, wheel, and censer. Green check at bottom.

1000. Vignette, Portrait of Chase, at bottom. Corners, at top black, with "1000;" below, on each side of Vignette, green, with "1000."

5000. Vignette, Indian girl, with bow leaning on shield, eagle near by. Left end, Justice. Corners, on left, green, with "5000," on right, green border with black centre, with "5000."

In the foregoing account of the various processes in the manufacture of a Bank Note, we have, in effect, described those employed by this Company in the production of the United States Treasury Notes. The imitations which we have given of one denomination of each kind, with the brief descriptions appended of the other denominations, will show their general character. Each combines all the safeguards against fraud now known. In speaking of the indestructible green ink used by the Company, we should have mentioned that it is used only on the face of the notes, its special use being, as has been explained, to guard against photographic counterfeits, by using in conjunction two inks of different colors, one of which can not be removed without removing the other. The photographic counterfeiter has nothing to gain by removing the check on the back. If he photographs it, the copy will appear in black. It can only be counterfeited by making an engraved imitation of the plate; and to guard against this, the most elaborate lathe-work has been lavished upon these backs. We repeat that our representations of the Treasury Notes are only imitations; they are not, and could not be made fac-similes of the genuine notes. It may not be uninteresting to compare them with the following perfect fac-simile of one of the Massachusetts Bills of 1690 —the first American paper money.

The Treasury "Demand Notes" have already become an important part of our currency. Being payable on presentation at the specified Branch Treasuries of the United States, they are equivalent to specie. The "Interest Notes" are due at the end of three years from date, with interest payable semi-annually. This interest, being at the rate of $7\frac{3}{10}$ per cent., amounts to just one cent a day upon every fifty dollars. To facilitate the payment of the interest, each

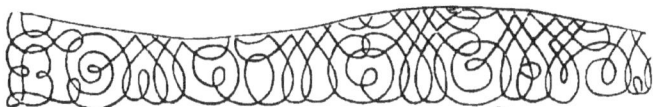

THIS Indented Bill of Twenty Shillings due from the Maſſachuſets Colony to the Poſſeſſor ſhall be in value equal to money & ſhall be accordingly accepted by the Treaſurer and Receivers ſubordinate to him in all Publick paym.ts and for any Stock at any time in the Treaſury. Boſton in New-England February the third 1690 By Order of the General Court

COUPONS.

of these notes has attached to it five little tickets, called "coupons," numbered in red to correspond with the note itself, and dated at intervals of six months. To collect the interest it is only necessary to cut off the coupon, and present it, when due, at any branch office of the Treasury. There are but five coupons for the three years, because the last installment, as specified on the note, is made payable with the note itself.

It was fortunate for the country that there was in existence an Association capable of executing these notes with the rapidity which was absolutely necessary. It would have taken months for the Government to have organized an establishment for this purpose. Machinery would have to be built, and hundreds of skilled workmen found; and then, after the expiration of a few months, the work would have been done, and the establishment must be disbanded. The "American Bank Note Company" was ready, at a week's notice, to put all the facilities which it had been accumulating for years at the disposal of the Government. Besides the main establishment in New York, which we have described, the Company has branches at Boston and Philadelphia, where the same operations are carried on. It had a similar branch at New Orleans at the time when our troubles broke out. This, for the present, is wholly lost. The entire organization is managed by a Board of Trustees, the President of which is the executive officer of the Company. Each Department is under the immediate direction of a competent superintendent; but all of them are directly accountable to the President, whose decision is final in all cases. Perfect harmony of action is thus secured in every branch of the organization.

All the various appliances which we have described are brought into play for the purpose of protecting the public from loss by spurious paper

money. We will devote a few paragraphs to a description of the different kinds of spurious paper, and the precautions which are or may be used against them.

1. *Counterfeits.*—By these we mean direct imitations of some genuine bill. To produce an even tolerable counterfeit demands an amount of artistic and mechanical talent which is rarely at the command of rogues. There is something in the artistic faculty which in most cases protects its possessor from temptations to fraud. It is only rarely that a good engraver turns out a rogue; moreover he can always do better by the honest exercise of his skill than by its fraudulent use. Now and then, indeed, a "dangerous" counterfeit is produced, and we wonder how and by whom it was made. But only a small part of the spurious money in circulation —probably not one dollar in twenty—is of this class. The security against counterfeits is found in the artistic execution of the genuine notes.— Of *Photographic Counterfeits*, and the precautions against them, we have spoken elsewhere.

2. *Raised Notes.*—These are genuine notes raised from a lower to a higher denomination— say from a "1" to a "10"—by altering the principal figures. This is sometimes done by removing the true figure, by means of which we have described, and printing in its place the larger one. More frequently, however, the altered figure is printed on thin paper and pasted over the true one. To guard against this, the denominational letters and figures should be so often repeated on each note as to render their erasure or concealment equivalent to making a new note. The general appearance of each denomination should also be wholly different. Some banks have the leading vignette repeated on all their notes. This is intended to guard against "Altered Notes," of which we shall

next speak. But we think the practice unwise. Vignettes, portraits, checks, and lettering should differ for every denomination.

3. *Altered Notes.*—These consist of the notes of some "bad" bank altered so as to represent those of a good one. Thus notes of the fraudulent "Bank of the Republic, Washington, D.C.," are altered so as to read "Bank of the Republic, New York." These alterations are either made by erasure and pasting on the notes themselves, or by altering parts of the plate itself and so printing them entirely new. Formerly too little care was taken of the plates. When a bank failed its assets, including the plates, were often sold at auction. These might fall into fraudulent hands, and be so altered as to represent notes of sound banks. The plates might have been executed in good faith by the best engravers, and there would be nothing in their general appearance to designate them as spurious. This class of frauds is the most usual and the most dangerous. To guard against these, every one whose business requires that he should have a "Counterfeit Detector," should also have the "Bank Note Descriptive List," containing brief descriptions of the character and positions of the principal parts of every genuine note. Whenever a note is offered with which he is not acquainted he should compare it with these descriptions. If it is an altered note they will differ essentially.

Bank Plates, moreover, should be kept with the utmost care. In fact, they should be considered as public property, the banks having only the right to their exclusive use for such number of impressions as they may legally issue. As

such, they should be in the custody of persons appointed by the State; and whenever a bank fails or retires from business the plates should be destroyed by the proper authority. This is done with the plates of banks under the New York General Banking Law. All these plates are in the custody of the Banking Department of the State. As it would be inconvenient and unsafe to send plates for this purpose to distant States, it would be far better for these States to make the Bank Note Company its sworn custodian for all plates. It has abundant means of guarding every plate; and its interest, as well as conscience, would impel it to the most perfect discharge of this duty. Indeed the Company now does all it can in this direction. Except in the case of banks of known and established character, it will not suffer the plates to leave its possession unless they are delivered to the authorities of States where there is a General Banking Law, similar to that of New York. If a bank at a distance should wish to stipulate for the delivery of its plates, it would, in ordinary cases, be considered as an indication that some improper use of them was intended, and the Company would decline to furnish the plates.

If the precautions which we have enumerated are carefully observed by the public, the danger of loss from spurious money will be so reduced that it need not be taken into the account in estimating the risks of business. The risk arising from broken banks belongs to a different category, and is to be guarded against only by wise and considerate action on the part of the public authorities by which these institutions are chartered.

www.ingramcontent.com/pod-product-compliance
Lightning Source LLC
Chambersburg PA
CBHW031455270326
41930CB00007B/1018